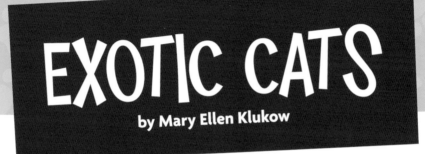

# EXOTIC CATS

by Mary Ellen Klukow

AMICUS | AMICUS INK

Amicus High Interest and Amicus Ink are published by Amicus
P.O. Box 1329, Mankato, MN 56002
www.amicuspublishing.us

Library of Congress Cataloging-in-Publication Data
Names: Klukow, Mary Ellen, author.
Title: Exotic cats / by Mary Ellen Klukow.
Description: Mankato, Minnesota : Amicus/Amicus Ink, [2020] | Series:
  Favorite cat breeds | Audience: K to Grade 3. | Includes index.
Identifiers: LCCN 2018048872 (print) | LCCN 2018049067 (ebook) | ISBN
  9781681518572 (pdf) | ISBN 9781681518176 (library binding) | ISBN
  9781681525457 (paperback)
Subjects: LCSH: Exotic shorthair cat—Juvenile literature. | Cat
  breeds—Juvenile literature.
Classification: LCC SF449.E93 (ebook) | LCC SF449.E93 K58 2020 (print) |
  DDC 636.8/2—dc23
LC record available at https://lccn.loc.gov/2018048872

Photo Credits: Shutterstock/ANCH cover; Shutterstock/LilKar 2; Alamy/
Katho Menden 5; Alamy/Martin Harvey 6; Alamy/Life on white 6;
Shutterstock/Chanita Chokchaikul 8–9, 10; Alamy/petographer 12–13,
18–19; Shutterstock/Vladislav Noseek 14–15; Shutterstock/Blanscape
16–17; iStock/yanjf 21; iStock/Volchanskiy 22

Editor: Alissa Thielges
Designer: Ciara Beitlich
Photo Researchers: Holly Young and Shane Freed

Printed in the United States of America

HC 10 9 8 7 6 5 4 3 2 1
PB 10 9 8 7 6 5 4 3 2 1

# TABLE OF CONTENTS

# POPULAR CAT

Look at that cat! He has a squished face and big round eyes. He is an Exotic Shorthair cat. This breed is the second most popular in the United States.

**Fun Fact**
The most popular cat breed in the United States is the Persian.

**Persian**

**Exotic Shorthair**

# NOT A PERSIAN

Exotics look like Persian cats. But Persians have long fur. An Exotic's fur is short. They are easier to **groom**. They are also more playful than Persians.

# MADE IN THE USA

The Exotic was created in the United States. It is a mix of Persian and American Shorthair cats. Both breeds are friendly and smart.

## Fun Fact
This breed is considered young. Exotics have only been around for 50 years.

# EXOTIC LOOK

Have you ever seen an Exotic?

They have a short, squashed nose.

Their round eyes are big and their

ears are small. They have short,

strong legs.

## Like a Wild Cat
Snow leopards have big eyes and small ears, too.

# KITTENS

Exotics usually have two or three kittens in a **litter**. This is less than **average**. Other cat breeds usually have three to five. Young kittens are active and playful.

# FAMILY CATS

Exotics are **social** cats. They like to be with their family. An Exotic might get **stressed** if it is left alone. They are much happier being around others.

# CUDDLE BUDDY

An Exotic's favorite place to be is on someone's lap. They love to **cuddle**. They watch TV with their family. They like to sleep with their family, too. Exotics love attention.

# SMART KITTIES

Exotics are smart. They can learn tricks. Some know "sit." Others can meow on command or stand on two feet. Some even know how to use a toilet!

## Like a Wild Cat?

Lions are smart, too. Female lions work together. They use a group hunting strategy to bring down large prey.

# SWEET PERSONALITY

Exotics make good pets. People love their personalities. They are sweet and smart. They get along with other pets. No wonder they are so popular.

# HOW DO YOU KNOW IT'S AN EXOTIC?

small ears

big, round eyes

round, squished face

thick tail with round tip

short legs

# WORDS TO KNOW

**average** – normal; what something usually is

**cuddle** – to hold or be held closely and lovingly

**groom** – to brush and clean

**litter** – a group of animals all born at the same time to the same mother

**social** – friendly and liking to be around other animals and people

**stressed** – being worried or feeling pressure that is uncomfortable

# LEARN MORE

## Books

Amstutz, Lisa. *Cats*. North Mankato, Minn.: Capstone Press, 2018.

Brown, Domini. *Exotics*. Minneapolis: Bellwether Media, 2016.

Finne, Stephanie. *Exotic Shorthair Cats*. Minneapolis: Abdo Publishing, 2015.

## Websites

**CFA: About the Exotic**
http://www.cfa.org/Breeds/BreedsCJ/Exotic.aspx

**Science Kids: Cats**
http://www.sciencekids.co.nz/sciencefacts/animals/cat.html

# INDEX